MAR   2015   SC1

D0623250

ZUMBA® Fitness

DANCE & FITNESS TRENDS

Michelle Medlock Adams

Mitchell Lane
PUBLISHERS
P.O. Box 196
Hockessin, DE 19707

Mitchell Lane
PUBLISHERS

African Dance Trends
Get Fit with Video Workouts
Line Dances Around the World
Trends in Hip-Hop Dance
Trends in Martial Arts
The World of CrossFit
Yoga Fitness
Zumba Fitness

PUBLISHER'S NOTE: The facts in this book have been thoroughly researched. Documentation of such research can be found on pages 44-45. While every possible effort has been made to ensure accuracy, the publisher will not assume liability for damages caused by inaccuracies in the data, and makes no warranty on the accuracy of the information contained herein.

The Internet sites referenced herein were active as of the publication date. Due to the fleeting nature of some web sites, we cannot guarantee that they will all be active when you are reading this book.

Printing
1   2   3   4   5   6   7   8   9

Library of Congress
Cataloging-in-Publication Data
Adams, Michelle Medlock.
  Zumba fitness / by Michelle Medlock Adams.
    pages cm. — (Dance and fitness trends)
  Includes bibliographical references and index.
  ISBN 978-1-61228-554-2 (library bound)
  1.   Aerobic dancing—Juvenile literature.
  2.   Aerobic exercise—Juvenile literature.   I.
Title.
  RA781.15.A34 2015
  613.7'15—dc 3
                        2014008301

Zumba®, Zumba® Fitness, Zumba® Kids, Zumba® Kids Jr., Zumba Gold®, Zumba® Gold-Toning, Aqua Zumba®, Zumba® Step, Zumba® in the Circuit, Zumba® Education Specialist, Zumba® Instructor Network, Zumba® Love, Zumbathon®, Zumbawear®, Ditch the Workout—Join the Party™, Zumba Sentao™, Zumbini™, ZIN™, Party in Pink™, The Great Calorie Drive™, and the Zumba Fitness logos are trademarks of Zumba Fitness, LLC, used under license.

eBook ISBN: 9781612285948

Contents

Introduction

With fourteen million weekly class participants in 185 countries, Zumba® (pronounced ZOOM-buh) Fitness is one of the most popular fitness programs today. It began in 2001—developed by fitness and dance instructor Beto Perez—and has been gaining momentum ever since. As Zumba instructors and faithful Zumba enthusiasts like to say, "Zumba is not just a workout, it's a way of life." Zumba Fitness is much more than a great way to burn calories, lose fat, and improve your cardiovascular health (though one study showed that you can torch up to 730 calories in an hour-long Zumba class). After all, many different fitness programs could boast of those merits. Zumba Fitness is a unique workout routine because it fuses fitness, entertainment, and fun into an all-out dance celebration.

So what exactly is Zumba? Simply put, it's a blend of rhythmic choreography with a Latin and world flavor that works your core and burns calories, all while you're dancing to upbeat music. Participants often dress in colorful workout wear or cargo pants during Zumba classes. A sassy form of dance combinations, Zumba makes you forget you're engaging in exercise. Instead, you're caught up in the music, trying to remember the sequence of hip-shaking steps, and dripping in sweat while loving every minute of it. Before you know it, you've danced your way through forty-five minutes of intense cardio. That's why people like Susan Sokeland, a certified Zumba instructor living and teaching in Southern Indiana, love it so much.

"I love to dance," she says, adding that she started taking Zumba classes in June 2010. "I prefer Zumba over other fitness classes because of its fun party atmosphere and Latin moves. I have taken Jazzercise and many other fitness classes. I liked them but it took Zumba to keep me committed."

Since beginning her Zumba journey, Susan has lost fifteen pounds, made many new friends, and even become certified to teach Zumba in April 2013. She teaches two Zumba classes a week at an area gym and has gained quite a following.

"I don't run a tight ship in my classes," she says, smiling. "I just keep it moving and encourage people to whoop it up and have fun. A lot of people like the rowdy party booty-shaking feel of Zumba. It lets people have fun while exercising, and there are very few programs that do this."

Zumba is also unique because participants range in age from newborns to seniors. Classes are offered for children (Zumba® Kids for ages seven to eleven, Zumba® Kids Jr. for ages four to six, and Zumbini™ for babies up to three years old and their caregivers) and seniors (Zumba Gold®). Zumba and its unique blend of fun and exercise truly offer something for everyone. And as the program continues to change and expand, its popularity is only growing!

Beto Perez, the inventor and founder of Zumba, leads a Latin-inspired Zumba class at Olympia Gym in Aventura, Florida.

Chapter 1
Beto Perez— Born to Dance

Alberto "Beto" Perez has always loved to dance. In fact, he spent almost every night of his childhood breakdancing in the streets of Cali, Colombia, with his friends. They learned from each other and challenged one another to be better, and Beto loved every minute of it. He felt the music with his heart and soul. But his mother was a deeply religious woman, and she didn't approve of his dancing.

Around the age of seven or eight, Beto watched the movie *Grease*. He began mimicking the dance numbers in the famous musical and adding a few steps of his own. He had potential, and he knew it in his heart, yet his family couldn't afford formal dance lessons. So Beto learned in other ways. As a teenager, he idolized Michael Jackson and became consumed with the King of Pop, his music, and the American pop and hip-hop culture. He studied Michael's moves and tried to imitate his fancy footwork. Still, his mother discouraged him. But one day Beto showed his mother a scene from the movie *Footloose*. In that scene, Ren McCormack (played by Kevin Bacon) quotes a passage from Ecclesiastes in the Bible, saying, ". . . and there is a time to dance." Finally, she came around and embraced his love of dance.

Then, when Beto was only fifteen, his mother was offered a good job in the United States. Beto didn't want his mom to turn down the opportunity, but he couldn't go with her, either. So he started working to show his mom that he would be fine without her. The many jobs he worked didn't leave him with much time for dance. But it was still in his heart.

Michael Jackson's dance moves were famous throughout the world. Teenage Beto studied these moves and taught himself to dance.

A Divine Mistake

Although Beto had no formal training, he had talent. He entered a lambada contest at nineteen years old, and he won. The Maria Sanford Brazilian Dance Academy in Cali gave him the opportunity to teach and study dance—but he had to teach step aerobics classes as well. It was a no-brainer for Beto. He finally received some instruction and continued growing as a dancer and a choreographer.

On one particular day, he arrived late to his aerobics class, and if that wasn't bad enough, he realized he had forgotten his aerobics music. So, he had no choice. He rummaged through his backpack and found a mix tape featuring club music—salsa and merengue tunes, specifically. Without any formal routines made up to those songs, Beto began leading the class in combinations of dance steps he did in the clubs on weekends, shaking his hips and pulsing to the rhythmic music. The participants loved it and caught on quickly. Soon everyone was dancing, sweating, and having a party in his aerobics class. Zumba Fitness was born.

A Meeting of the Minds in Miami

With only his dreams and his magnificent moves, twenty-nine-year-old Beto sold all of his belongings and headed for Miami in 1999. He didn't speak any English, but his dancing spoke volumes and could break down any language barrier. He secured a job teaching fitness in Miami, and one of his faithful followers just happened to be the mother of Alberto Perlman, a gutsy entrepreneur. Having heard his mother rave about Beto's classes, Perlman decided to sit in on one of Beto's classes and see for himself. He was not disappointed. "There are 120 people, packed in like sardines," he told *Inc.* magazine. "They are screaming and smiling. No one looks tired. No one is showing any pain. I thought, 'We've got to do something with this.'"

At the time, Perlman was trying to make a comeback after suffering some major setbacks in his own business affairs, and the possibilities of this new fitness craze excited him. Another Alberto—Alberto Aghion—had worked for one of Perlman's companies that went under and was also looking for work. So, as fate would have it, there was a meeting of the minds with

Zumba Fitness Founders—the three Albertos: Alberto "Beto" Perez (left), Alberto Perlman (center), and Alberto Aghion (right)—take time for a snapshot at the Zumba headquarters.

the three Albertos—Alberto "Beto" Perez, Alberto Perlman, and Alberto Aghion. They decided that Beto definitely had a marketable product and made plans to shoot a video of one of his classes.

With two hundred pumped participants and Beto's brand of booty-shaking fitness, they shot a video of his class on a beautiful beach near Miami. The team of Albertos showed the video to the CEO of Fitness Quest, and he was impressed. Months later, Fitness Quest released a series of tapes and DVDs and sold them with an infomercial. They did well—selling about a million copies in six months—but the call center kept hearing the same thing over and over. People wanted to know how they could attend a real class.

Can Fitness Be Fun and Effective?

With its slogan, "Ditch the Workout—Join the Party!™" Zumba has taken the fitness world by storm and brought fun back into the gym, but is it actually an effective form of exercise?

That's what fitness experts at the American Council on Exercise wanted to know, so they asked researchers John Porcari and Mary Luettgen of the University of Wisconsin-La Crosse to find out. Specifically, this Workout Watchdog® team wanted to test the average exercise intensity and energy output during a typical Zumba class, so they recruited nineteen women, ages eighteen to twenty-two. The women were healthy and experienced in Zumba, but were all at different levels of fitness. They used monitors to track the participants' heart rates, oxygen consumption, and calories burned.

Here's what they discovered:

» Zumba is a total body workout, especially good for strengthening the core and improving flexibility because of the hip movements.

» Zumba burns more calories than cardio kickboxing, step aerobics, hooping, and power yoga. Participants in the study burned between seven and twelve calories per minute.

» No matter what your fitness level—in poor shape or quite fit—Zumba provides a great cardio workout. All of the women in the study, fit or not, were working out in the heart rate zone that improves cardio health.

» You don't have to get every step just right in order to get a good workout.

So, yes it's a party, but it's a party that's going to kick your butt!

Zumba is an international craze. Here future Zumba instructors participate in a Zumba Basic Instructor Training in Moscow, Russia.

Chapter 2
Zumba Instructors Are Born

If classes were what the people wanted, then the three Albertos were going to find a way to give them just that—Zumba classes with instructors leading the same Latin-influenced dance parties that Beto brought to his classes. So, they put out the word that they would be leading the very first Zumba training session for fitness instructors in a Miami hotel in 2003, calling it "Zumba Academy." They thought 30 or 40 people would attend, but instead, over 150 people showed up to become certified Zumba instructors. They flew in from as far away as California and Kansas! The three Albertos knew they were onto something.

Seven hundred Zumba instructors had been trained by 2005, and the love for this Latin-inspired dance party was spreading to gyms across the United States and around the world, according to *Inc.* magazine. By May 2010, there were more than twenty thousand Zumba instructors in seventy-five countries. And that number has only continued to multiply.

Certification classes started popping up all over the world, and fitness enthusiasts were leaving each seminar with a new Zumba certification, new moves for their classes, a new career, and a new network of support and friends. For $30 a month, every Zumba instructor was encouraged to join ZIN™ (Zumba® Instructor Network) which granted access to online marketing tools, continuing education, choreography DVDs, music, and the latest news regarding Zumba and community support.

The 411 on How to Become an Instructor

Can you imagine getting paid to work out, burn calories, have fun, and dance with a lot of fabulous people? Well, that's what instructors get to do every single time they lead a Zumba class. Becoming a Zumba instructor today is simple. Once you have attended one of the Zumba Instructor Trainings, you also need to maintain your license and build a following for your classes.

You don't need to have any other fitness training to earn a Zumba instructor certification, but you should be acquainted with this form of exercise. In other words, before you embark on the instructor's journey, you should attend Zumba classes in your community. Make sure you take classes from different instructors so you can experience a wide variety of routines and combinations. Try to attend at least three Zumba classes each week to prepare for your Zumba certification.

The next thing you need to do is decide which Zumba license you want. You can choose from Zumba Basic Level 1 or the Jump Start Gold Instructor Training. In the Zumba Basic training (which is an excellent place to begin your instructor's journey), you will learn the foundational steps of Zumba, which are done to four types of music: reggaeton, salsa, cumbia, and merengue. By the time you finish your training, you'll understand how to create choreography for your own classes using these basic Zumba steps. With the Jump Start Gold Instructor Training, you'll learn the Zumba Basic information, and you'll also learn how to lead Zumba at a level appropriate for older adults. The fee for each certification ranges from $225 to $340, and the license you receive is good for a year of instruction. Once you have your license, you should also take a First Aid, AED, and CPR certification course. These are offered in most areas by organizations like the American Red Cross for around $50 to $100.

You may be thinking, "Well, I'm too young to be a Zumba instructor." Although the requirements state that you must be

In Poland, an instructor leads students in high-energy, Latin-inspired moves called Zumba. This outdoor class was held for people celebrating the Polish holiday of Juwenalia.

eighteen years old to receive a license, there is an exception. If you are sixteen or seventeen, you simply need a letter from one of your parents and a signed liability form to participate in the Zumba Instructor Training. And if you're younger than that, you can still take regular Zumba classes to practice and prepare for the future.

Catalina Mejia, pictured above leading class, has been certified by Guinness World Records as the youngest Zumba instructor in the world.

When seventeen-year-old Cata Mejia first received her license, however, there was no age limit. She has been teaching Zumba for the past six years and loving every minute of it! Becoming a certified instructor in 2007 at age eleven earned Cata the title of "Youngest Zumba Instructor in the World" from Guinness World Records. Though she couldn't officially "work" at such a young age, Cata taught Zumba classes for free at birthday parties and community and charity events. In fact, in 2011 she helped raise $758 for charity by teaching at a two-hour Zumba event called a Zumbathon®.

For Cata, it was love at first hip shake. She fell head over sneakers for Zumba and its Latin and world dance movements when she accompanied her mother to a Zumba class about an hour away from their home. Once the music began, and Cata felt it pulsating through her veins, she was hooked.

She told writer Jennipher Walters of *Shape* that she doesn't just like Zumba, she loves it! "The reason is simple: It's a great way to exercise while having fun, it's for absolutely everyone, and it's an amazing way to bring people together through something they like," Cata explained. "It also has a positive vibe to it."

Zumba was a game changer for Cata. It put her on a path that she had never imagined. She told *Shape*, "My goal is to influence as many people as I can to live a healthy lifestyle while having fun, to never give up and follow their dreams, and to go above and beyond what they think they can do."

Her plans? Finish college, become a Zumba® Education Specialist, and open her very own dance studio.

If you plan to attend a Zumba Instructor Training, make sure you take a towel, a water bottle, a sweatshirt, a healthy snack, a lunch, Zumba shoes or fitness shoes, a notepad and pen, and a positive attitude. Like it was for Cata, the Zumba Instructor Training might be a game changer for you!

Why I Became a Zumba Instructor

I began taking dance lessons at Rusty LaVonne's Dance Studio in Bedford, Indiana, when I was only four years old, so I grew up tapping, doing ballet and jazz, and loving all of it. As soon as I could try out for the cheerleading squad and dance teams at school, I also did that. I cheered for the Parkview Panthers, the Bedford Middle School Stone Cutters, and the Bedford North Lawrence High School (BNLHS) Stars. I was also part of the award-winning Starsteppers Dance Team at BNLHS. Dance and cheerleading were both huge parts of my life, and so was keeping in shape—both of those sports required stamina and form-fitting uniforms.

I remember waking up early before school to exercise with the Jane Fonda workout videos—leg warmers and all. Fast forward to my freshman year of college. I was cheering at Asbury University, but I wanted to take on a part-time job to earn a little spending money. A cousin of mine was a certified fitness instructor and told me about an upcoming fitness certification weekend. She suggested that I attend so I could become certified and then teach aerobics at the college. It sounded like a good plan to me, so I did just that. I really enjoyed teaching dance aerobics and earning a little money along the way.

I taught dance aerobics, cardiofunk, step aerobics, and toning classes most of my life . . . and then a friend of mine invited me to try Zumba one day at a nearby dance studio. She said, "I think it's something you're going to love because you get to shake your booty." With an invitation like that, who could say no? She was right; I did love it. I enjoyed every sweaty minute of that Zumba class. After about six months of attending faithfully, I decided to get my Zumba certification in 2011. Today, I make up most of my routines and mix music from the official Zumba CDs with popular music for an hour-long, hip-shaking, high-energy kind of class. I am always mixing it up, but one thing remains the same—we always have fun.

Zumba appeals to many people because it's easy to follow and fun to do, as this young woman learned in 2014.

Chapter 3
The Beat Goes On

Never in Beto's wildest dreams did he imagine that his mix of hip-hop, samba, salsa, mambo, cha-cha, reggaeton, Bollywood, belly dancing, tango, and more would become a fitness craze that would eventually attract numerous celebrities. Jennifer Lopez, Kirstie Alley, Jackie Chan, Natalie Portman, Emma Watson, Victoria Beckham, Halle Berry, Toni Braxton, Nicky Hilton, and Wyclef Jean have all incorporated Zumba into their workouts. Beto couldn't have known, either, that his brand of fitness would spread to 185 countries or be named the "Company of the Year" by *Inc*. magazine in 2012. But all of those amazing things have happened, and even more continue to unfold.

A Bit More History

From chapter two, we know that the three Albertos began training Zumba instructors and the brand grew. They trademarked Zumba and pledged to expand it all over the world, which they have done through a wide variety of business ventures. After the success of the DVDs and the Zumba Instructor Trainings, demand arose for Zumba music CDs, giving Zumba instructors and participants a way to "party at home" to their own Zumba music. But that wasn't enough . . . the growth continued. In 2010, Zumba released a video game for each of the three major gaming platforms—Wii, Xbox 360, and PlayStation 3—the first fitness brand to do so. It seemed like one Zumba idea spurred another. The fitness brand simply exploded and began dominating various industries—especially in the area of music.

Music artists and labels have discovered that Zumba is a powerful tool for getting their music to fans. Daddy Yankee's reggaeton hit "Limbo" was written for Zumba Fitness classes.

Since music is the highlight of any Zumba class, it seemed only natural when Zumba began creating its own songs. Artists like Wyclef Jean, Pitbull, and Don Omar have also collaborated with the fitness company to release and promote their songs on Zumba's CD compilations. In 2012, *Billboard* magazine predicted that Zumba could be "the next music platform" for artists and their songs to reach listeners. This new platform has already had remarkable success with number-one hits like "Limbo" by Daddy Yankee and Don Omar's "Zumba."

As the former chairman and CEO of MTV Networks International William Roedy shared with *Inc.*, "It's hotter than MTV in any of the hot years I saw MTV. They have this perfect synergy with music that is great for the whole industry."

Major record companies are noticing as well. Alberto Perlman told *Inc.* that he's received phone calls from Universal, EMI, and Sony, all wanting to know, "Can we put this song we're launching out on the ZIN network?" They know about fourteen million people will hear it if they do. He also shared that music artists are saying, "I don't need a record label. I'll just put my song up on iTunes, and Zumba can be my promotional vehicle."

Obviously, Zumba is a force to be reckoned with in many areas—even in the fitness apparel industry. As the number of Zumba instructors and participants grew, the demand grew for Zumba clothing. That prompted the three Albertos to develop and market bright and colorful Zumbawear® apparel and accessories, catering to the party atmosphere of the classes. "Clothing is a big thing for us. The demand is unstoppable," Alberto Perlman told *Business Insider*. "Everyone is wearing black yoga pants and then you see the Zumba people wearing colorful, cool cargo pants. It makes a statement that says 'I don't have to hide like everyone else. I can show a little bit of brightness, and not have to wear these black pants.'"

Customers obviously agree—they buy more than 3.5 million pieces of Zumbawear clothing every year.

Zumbawear, shown here, is different from typical fitness clothing. Zumba enthusiasts love the bright, colorful workout wear.

Obstacles Along the Way

Like many great ideas in their early stages, Zumba faced obstacles along the road to success. Not everyone embraced this new form of fitness—especially some of the "major players" in the fitness world. Before Zumba became mainstream, it was rejected by many of the big gym chains.

"They wouldn't hire our instructors for many years," Alberto Perlman told *Business Insider*. So Zumba instructors took their exciting classes to the smaller gyms, community centers,

dance studios, and school gymnasiums. The people found them anyway. Zumba didn't need the backing of the big gyms because the people wanted it so badly they'd drive to wherever class was being held just to take part in the fitness party.

Within three years, those same gyms that initially rejected Zumba were calling Perlman and asking how they could get involved. Turns out, Zumba didn't need the big gyms—the big gyms needed Zumba.

At first, many American gyms did not want to offer Zumba classes to their members. Zumba classes are now held in the United States and around the world. In this 2011 photo, more than 1,200 participants dance with instructors in Brownsville, Texas.

Perlman believes that others can learn from Zumba's story. "Don't listen to the big corporations or the big business people—listen to the consumers," he told *Business Insider*. "If you know your product is good and consumers like your product, it doesn't matter what anyone else says."

That same positive outlook has driven Zumba to bigger and better things every single year since its debut. Don't expect the brand's growth to fizzle out any time soon—it continues to evolve, grow, and expand as the market changes.

So Many Zumba Classes,
So Little Time

When the Zumba empire was just beginning, only the basic Zumba class was available. Still, that was enough to inspire thousands of men and women to work out and have fun at the same time. Since its beginnings, though, Zumba has found ways to expand its class lineup.

Currently, there are several different types of Zumba classes, and more options are constantly being developed. Instructors need a separate certification for each type of class that they want to teach.

The current class types are:

» Zumba Gold: a low-impact workout for older adults
» Zumba Kids: a class designed for children ages seven to twelve
» Zumba Kids Jr.: a class designed for children ages four to six
» Zumbini: a class designed for babies three years old and under and their caregivers
» Zumba® Toning: a workout using toning sticks—light hand weights that are used to help tone the body
» Zumba® Gold-Toning: a modified, slower-paced toning class for older adults
» Aqua Zumba®: Zumba in a swimming pool
» Zumba Sentao™: a chair workout that focuses on using body weight to strengthen and tone the body
» Zumba® Step: combines step aerobics with Zumba's dance moves for a power workout for the lower body
» Zumba® in the Circuit: a high-energy dance/ fitness workout combined with strength training

Most classes are $5 to $15 per class unless your gym membership includes all classes in your monthly membership fee.

Zumba fitness instructor Nancy Hills proudly shows off her size 22 jeans during the annual Zumbalicious Dance Party at the Highland Complex in Largo, Florida. Through fitness and diet, Nancy says she is now wearing a size 6.

Chapter 4
The Many Benefits of Zumba

We know that Zumba provides a great cardiovascular workout. It has also been known to help its participants lose unwanted pounds, tone up, and have fun all at the same time. But, there are other benefits as well—benefits Beto never anticipated.

Take one faithful participant in West Yorkshire, England, named Diane West. She explained to *The Telegraph* that each week, "I see a group of tired, ordinary women come to life. Whether it's the music or the moves, the change is undeniable. There's a J-Lo or Beyoncé inside all these women—it's total, powerful, mind-blowing energy."

And Diane isn't the only Zumba faithful to describe the workout as empowering, energizing, and mind-blowing. It seems that many people who lack self-confidence are able to "come to life" once the music begins and they join their friends in an hour of dance.

Zumba has become "the place to be" and "the place to belong." Many participants are finding that friendship and support are two of the biggest benefits. Angie Williams Johnson is a forty-six-year-old fitness enthusiast in Southern Indiana who has been working out for about eight years. But it wasn't until she started attending Zumba classes three years ago that she became consistent with her workouts and actually wanted to go to the gym. "I keep coming back because it is fun," she said, "and because the others who do it motivate me, too."

They cheer each other on. They celebrate every pound lost. They give hugs when someone is facing a challenge. They laugh with each other as they try to learn new choreography. They bond over Latin music every single class. Angie said she

Angie Williams Johnson, who regularly participates in Zumba classes at Priority Fitness in Bedford, Indiana, says she has lost pounds and gained friends since discovering Zumba three years ago.

is thankful for the great friends she has made through Zumba. When the music stops, their friendships continue inside and outside the gym.

"I love to participate," Angie added. "And, I love the people I have met while doing Zumba."

Feeling Good with Zumba

When a person engages in certain types of exercise, his or her body releases endorphins. These "feel-good" chemicals are known for giving runners what is often referred to as a "runner's high." And Zumba participants are experiencing that same feel-good state in an equally dramatic way.

United Kingdom-based Zumba instructor Nicola Swindle told *The Telegraph* that a Zumba class exercises both your endorphins and your muscles. "I focused on the health and fitness benefits of the class to begin with," she explained, noting that Zumba is exercise in disguise. "But now I'm beginning to think it's Prozac in disguise as well."

Zumba CEO Alberto Perlman agreed. "It's the only real fitness program where most people taking it are not taking it for the fitness benefits," he told *Business Insider*. "They're taking it for the happiness and joy that they feel while they're doing it, and the fitness is just a result of this."

He added, "We know so many people who have gone off their depression medications because of Zumba. . . . A person that is depressed and on Prozac . . . this is one hour when they're not on their meds. If you have breast cancer, it's one hour when you don't remember that you have it."

Breast cancer survivor and Zumba instructor Michelle Lombardo can attest to the truth of Perlman's statement. She taught her Zumba classes full time at her studio Wicked Z and Dance Fitness in Rocky Hill, Connecticut, while she was being treated for cancer.

"Teaching my Zumba classes was an integral part of my healing process throughout my treatment regimen," Michelle told *The Philippine Star*. "Zumba saved my life in many ways. Just knowing that throughout my treatment, I could still teach Zumba classes and the inspiration that my students say they get from me when in fact I do the classes because I get inspired by them. The joy that you get teaching people, the joy that you get doing the program is a blessing."

Michelle isn't alone in her experience. Diana Walton of Hawaii has been a Zumba instructor since 2008. She's also a survivor of stage four breast cancer. Doctors told Diana that she would not live. But Diana was a fighter and she decided to attack her disease head-on. Part of her motivation came from the Zumba classes she taught.

"I am in Hawaii because I am a military wife," Diana shared with *The Philippine Star*. "I took pills doctors gave me after the surgery for the first three months and then I just went green and exercised. And I said, 'I am not going to die. I am going to fight.' It has been five years since I was diagnosed in 2009. The Zumba classes I teach in Hawaii are massive. I have two hundred students in every class. When they see the joy in my face and my big hair, they ask me if I am a survivor. And I gleefully say yes. Life is full of joy and happiness, and Zumba has done this to me."

Zumba classes are fun and fast-moving.

Zumba participants in Susan Sokeland's class at Priority Fitness in Bedford, Indiana, prove that fitness can be fun.

As Beto told *Reader's Digest*, "I think people in the fitness business create programs for people in the fitness world. With Zumba, anyone can do it." He and his partners created a fitness program for the everyday people—the students who couldn't afford fancy gym equipment at home, the tired moms who needed some time just for themselves, kids who've never taken a dance class, the overweight people who were afraid they might be judged in other fitness classes, and the people fighting mental health issues and life-threatening diseases who wanted to escape their pain for an hour. For those people and so many others, Zumba has been a lifesaver. Its benefits reach far beyond the physical, healing hearts and restoring hope one class at a time.

Why They Love Zumba!

» *Lacey Johnson Wagner, twenty-eight-year-old qualification scientist at a Navy base and Zumba substitute instructor:* I think Zumba has become so popular because it's so fun and you don't feel like you are working out while doing it.

» *Angela Edwards, certified Zumba instructor for the past four years:* I like this much better than any other fitness class I have been to. I love to dance and I really don't realize it's a workout while doing it.

» *Susan Sokeland, certified Zumba instructor:* I lead Zumba for fun and exercise and to make friends. I have achieved all of those goals. I have a wide circle of friends due to Zumba, and I think many people can say the same thing.

Lacey Johnson Wagner

Zumba enthusiasts love to attend classes, but it's even better when the class benefits charity! Zumbathons are held all over the world each year, and raise money for causes like breast cancer prevention and heart health.

Zumba Gives Back

You give Zumba an hour each class, and it gives back to you in big ways as we've discovered in the previous chapters of this book—through weight loss, a toned physique, a renewed sense of self, a more energetic attitude, new friends, and more. The gifts just continue to multiply, right?

Well, Zumba also continues to give back on a large scale through Zumba® Love. The mission of Zumba Love, according to the official Zumba website, "is to foster charitable initiatives that raise funds and awareness for important causes, and to celebrate the joy of giving through dance, fitness, friendship, and love."

The passion that fuels the Zumba program also inspires and attracts passionate, caring instructors and fans all around the world. While Zumba has healing properties all of its own, Zumba Love also gives instructors and students the opportunity to help heal others by raising money for medical research. Instructors have so far held over nine thousand Zumbathon charity events and raised millions of dollars for breast cancer research, motor neuron disease research, heart health, childhood obesity, and more.

Powerful in Pink

Zumba Fitness launched the Party in Pink™ charity campaign in 2010 to help in the fight against breast cancer. In the program's first three years, over $3 million was raised for Susan G. Komen®, a charity dedicated to ending breast cancer forever. Initially, donations were coming from all over the world, but the money was going to American institutions. That didn't

Party in Pink Zumbathons are held each year to raise money for breast cancer prevention. Often, several instructors team up to attract more participants to these extra-long "parties with a purpose."

seem fair to the overseas Zumba instructors and fans who were working hard at these charity events, too. That caused Alberto Perlman to rethink the Pink initiative.

"What if we discover something new that will benefit people all around the world?" he suggested to *The Philippine Star*. Instead of funding research for new medications, in 2013 Zumba Fitness decided to channel all of the future Party in Pink funds to breast cancer prevention research. Finding a way to prevent breast cancer would have a global rather than a local impact. The new grant is managed by Susan G. Komen, and Zumba Fitness guaranteed a minimum donation of $3 million from 2013 to 2015.

The Party in Pink Zumbathons, which run between July 15 and October 31 each year, have already been remarkably successful. Whether for treatment or prevention, the goal of these events was to raise at least $1 million each year for Susan G. Komen. Party in Pink attendees can be sure that their donations will be used for research. Today, seventy-five percent of the price of each ticket sold is donated to the Zumba Global Research Grant for Breast Cancer Prevention. Fans can also purchase limited-edition Party in Pink Zumbawear, knowing that 30 cents of each dollar goes directly to breast cancer prevention research. Neither Zumba nor Susan G. Komen deduct any fees from the donations.

According to the Komen organization, such a large and consistent contribution is rare, even among big companies. American Airlines has been the only other company to raise at least $1 million each year for research through Susan G. Komen. "Every company can donate money to the cause, but Zumba changes lives—especially for cancer patients and survivors," Alberto Perlman told *The Philippine Star*. "Some women with breast cancer tell us they are very self-conscious about how they look physically and that Zumba . . . helps them develop the attitude that they need to fight this tragic disease."

The Great Calorie Drive™

From March 1 to June 30, 2013, Zumba Fitness gave participants a way to "donate" the calories they burned at their classes to hungry people around the world. Each time someone checked into a class using the Zumba Fitness mobile app (up to three times total), Zumba donated $0.14, to the World Food Programme and Feeding America. While $0.14 might not seem like a lot, these organizations used that money to provide 750 calories of food (or more) to hungry people in the United States and around the world. According to the final tally, Zumba participants donated 82,107,750 calories during the 2013 campaign.

That meant a lot to Beto, because he grew up in the poverty-stricken nation of Colombia. At an instructor conference in Lille, France, he introduced The Great Calorie Drive™ to a room full of Zumba instructors, journalists, and staff. He said the fundraiser was important to him because, "I was very poor as a kid. And when I tell people about my childhood, people

The Great Calorie Drive helped the World Food Programme to deliver food to the people who need it most, like this woman in Burundi.

are surprised. . . . But I lived it. . . . I remember when we didn't have food." Beto explained that as a teenager in Colombia, he worked all day for a glass of milk and a banana.

In a video shown at the conference, Lil Wayne encouraged Zumba instructors and participants to join together to "give the world a reason to dance!" And that's really the heart behind Zumba Love. To date, Zumba Love has donated more than $7 million to charities, including Susan G. Komen and its global nonprofit partners, the American Heart Association, Augie's Quest (to end ALS, or Lou Gehrig's disease), and more. And, according to Beto, it's only the beginning. There's much work left to do.

So You Want to Make a Difference? Party with a Purpose!

If you'd like to get involved with a Zumba Love event or another charitable event sponsored by a licensed Zumba instructor, the best place to start is online. Go to http://www.zumba.com/en-US/about/love, where you can learn about upcoming events and read about the positive impact Zumba Love is making around the world.

From "Movin' for Parkinson's" to "Benefit for the Bayou," Zumba Love has put its best charitable foot forward in order to make a difference. You can do your part by signing up for a nearby Zumbathon. If you can't find one in your local area, ask your instructor to host a Zumba charity event for your favorite cause. You may even be able to help by setting up for the class or by spreading the word. So, join the party and party with a purpose!

- Before beginning any fitness program, you'll want to check with your parents and your doctor to make sure you are physically ready to "get your Zumba on." After getting their blessing, you might want to learn a few of the basic Zumba moves so you won't feel overwhelmed when you attend your first official Zumba class. The best ways to learn Zumba at home are with DVDs, Zumba video games, and YouTube instructional videos such as this basic steps video: https://www.youtube.com/watch?v=irptqdkJ1lU.

- Check with your local fitness facilities, gyms, schools, churches, and YMCA to see if they offer any Zumba classes. They might even have a Zumba class just for kids, so ask. Don't forget to check your local community calendar, as well, because many cities have Zumba programs in place. If you're specifically looking for Aqua Zumba, it's a good idea to check with your local pools to see if they have an Aqua Zumba program in operation. If they don't, why not suggest one? You can also go to Zumba.com and type your address into the "Find a Class" box. You will be taken to a full list of Zumba classes in your area.

- It's important to wear appropriate clothing when participating in Zumba, just like with any other workout. Zumba offers an entire line of fitness wear in bright colors. You can check it out at http://www.zumba.com/en-US/store/US/. Just be sure to ask your parents' permission before ordering any Zumbawear. And don't feel like you have to wear Zumba clothing in order to participate in a Zumba class. Just make sure you are able to move comfortably—leggings, shorts, or sweatpants with a fitted tank/sports bra and a loose coverup or t-shirt will work for girls. Shorts, sweatpants, or track pants with a t-shirt or tank top are good options for guys. You'll see everything from running shorts and t-shirts to belly-dance outfits with hip scarves. Even more important than your clothing is the right kind of shoe. You may have great running or fitness shoes, but those might not be your best bet for a Zumba class. You'll want a shoe that can slide easily to keep time with the beats. If your fitness shoe has too much grip on the bottom, it will hinder your movement. Try some steps on a hard floor at home to see if you can move easily, or if the shoe sticks to the floor too much. You should choose a shoe with good shock absorption since many of the dance moves involve impact. This will help protect your knees and ankles as you execute salsa and merengue moves in class. You can also ask your instructor what kind of shoes they recommend, since every class is a little different!

- Whether you're looking for the nearest licensed Zumba instructor, trying to find out how to become a Zumba instructor, or simply wanting to buy the latest, greatest Zumbawear, just go to http://www.zumba.com/en-US online and follow the very simple menu.

1990s	Alberto "Beto" Perez arrives to teach his aerobics class in Cali, Colombia, and realizes he has forgotten his aerobics tape. He improvises and uses some of the Latin music he has in his backpack, winging the whole class. The students love every minute of it, and Zumba is accidentally born.
1999	After his success in Colombia, Beto Perez brings his booty-shaking brand of Latin fitness to the United States.
2001	Beto meets entrepreneurs Alberto Perlman and Alberto Aghion, and they create a global company based on Beto's fitness brand.
2002	The Albertos secure a deal with a large fitness company and sell about one million videos with infomercials.
2003	The three Albertos create a Zumba instructor training program and host the first one in Miami, calling it "Zumba Academy." Over 150 instructors arrive from all over the country.
2005	There are approximately seven hundred trained Zumba instructors.
2007	Zumba spans all six populated continents—North America, South America, Europe, Africa, Asia and Australia. Now, the entire world has joined the fitness party!
2010	Zumba releases a video game for Wii, Xbox 360, and PlayStation 3, becoming the first fitness company to release a game on the three major gaming platforms. Zumba Love is formed to give back, launching the Party in Pink charity campaign to help in the fight against breast cancer.
2012	*Billboard* predicts that Zumba is the next music platform. Zumba Fitness is named "Company of the Year" by *Inc.* magazine.
2013	The Party in Pink campaign is changed—now it benefits breast cancer prevention research, which has a global impact.
2014	Zumba is featured on ABC's *Extreme Weight Loss* show, following Charita Smith on her weight loss journey and life transformation. Viewers see how Zumba can make a difference in a person's life in the May 27 episode. Smith eventually becomes a Zumba instructor.

Further Reading

Books

Perez, Beto, and Maggie Greenwood-Robinson. *Zumba: Ditch the Workout, Join the Party! The Zumba Weight Loss Program.* New York: Hachette Book Group, 2009.

On the Internet

Inc. Live: "Zumba: How We Built a Global Fitness Empire" http://www.inc.com/zumba/zumba-fitness-how-we-built-a-global-fitness-empire.html

Walters, Jennipher. "Meet Cata, the Youngest Zumba Instructor in the World." *Shape*, May 29, 2012. http://www.shape.com/blogs/shape-your-life/meet-cata-youngest-zumba-instructor-world

YouTube: "Zumba Kids" https://www.youtube.com/watch?v=kiRpnDeAOlI

Works Consulted

Ballestier, Courtney. "Why She Loves Beto Perez: Zumba Fitness." *Men's Fitness*. http://www.mensfitness.com/training/cardio/why-she-loves-beto-perez-zumba-fitness

Buchanan, Leigh. "Zumba Fitness: Company of the Year." *Inc.*, December 4, 2012. http://www.inc.com/magazine/201212/leigh-buchanan/zumba-fitness-company-of-the-year-2012.html

Cobo, Leila. "Body Rock: Is Zumba the Next Music Platform?" *Billboard*, June 22, 2012. http://www.billboard.com/biz/articles/news/1093057/body-rock-is-zumba-the-next-music-platform

Dunnell, Jasmin. "The Best Shoes to Wear to Zumba Class." BestExerciseShoes.com. http://bestexerciseshoes.com/shoes-to-wear-to-zumba/

Edwards, Angela (Certified Zumba instructor in Bedford, Indiana). Email interview with the author, January 2014.

El Mallah, Amina. "The Great Calorie Drive™—Help End World Hunger before June 30th!" *TheZumbaBlog.com*, June 4, 2013. http://www.thezumbablog.com/2013/06/04/the-great-calorie-drive-help-end-world-hunger-before-june-30th/

Giang, Vivian. "How Zumba Became the Largest Fitness Brand in the World." *Business Insider*, December 31, 2012. http://www.businessinsider.com/how-zumba-became-the-largest-fitness-brand-in-the-world-2012-12?op=1#ixzz2q4kRcvH7

The Great Calorie Drive. http://www.greatcaloriedrive.com/en/site/

Johnson, Angela Williams (Zumba participant in Bedford, Indiana). Email interview with the author, January 2014.

Luettgen, Mary, John Porcari, Carl Foster, Richard Mikat, and Jose Rodriguez-Morroyo. "Zumba Fitness: Sure It's Fun But Is It Effective?" *ACE Certified News*, September 2012. http://www.acefitness.org/certifiednewsarticle/2813/

Market Watch, Wall Street Journal. "'Party, Prevent, Prevail': Zumba's 'Party in Pink (TM)' Initiative to Fund the Zumba(R) Global Research Grant for Breast Cancer Prevention in Partnership with Susan G. Komen(R)." July 30, 2013. http://www.marketwatch.com/story/party-prevent-prevail-zumbas-party-in-pinktm-initiative-to-fund-the-zumbar-global-research-grant-for-breast-cancer-prevention-in-partnership-with-susan-g-komenr-2013-07-30

Mendoza-Dayrit, Mylene. "Cancer Patients Zumba Their Way to Healing." *Philippine Star*, August 27, 2013. http://www.philstar.com/health-and-family/2013/08/27/1137061/cancer-patients-zumba-their-way-healing

Perez, Beto, and Maggie Greenwood-Robinson. *Zumba: Ditch the Workout, Join the Party! The Zumba Weight Loss Program.* New York: Hachette Book Group, 2009.

Reader's Digest. "Meet the Man Behind Zumba: Beto Perez." November 2009. http://www.rd.com/advice/work-career/meet-the-man-behind-zumba-beto-perez/

Sokeland, Susan (Certified Zumba Instructor in Bedford, Indiana). Email interview with the author, January 2014.

Susan G. Komen. "Zumba's 'Party in Pink™' Initiative to Fund the Zumba® Global Research Grant for Breast Cancer Prevention in Partnership with Susan G. Komen®" July 30, 2013. http://ww5.komen.org/KomenNewsArticle.aspx?id=19327356968

Wagner, Lacey (Zumba substitute teacher in Bedford, Indiana). Email interview with the author, January 2014.

Walters, Jennipher. "Meet Cata, the Youngest Zumba Instructor in the World." *Shape,* May 29, 2012. http://www.shape.com/blogs/shape-your-life/meet-cata-youngest-zumba-instructor-world

Weinberg, Kate. "Zumba Your Troubles Away." *Telegraph*, May 14, 2010 http://www.telegraph.co.uk/active/7723739/Zumba-your-troubles-away.html

Zumba Costa Blanca. "History of Zumba." http://www.zumbacostablanca.com/about/history-of-zumba/

Zumba Fitness. "Company Snapshot." http://www.zumba.com/en-US/about

Zumba Fitness. "Zumba Love: Movin' for Charity." http://www.zumba.com/en-US/about/love

atmosphere (AT-muhs-feer)—The mood or feeling of a place and time.

certification (sur-tuh-fi-KEY-shuhn)—The state of having a certificate (or other verification) which proves that a course has been completed.

choreography (kohr-ee-OG-ruh-fee)—Rhythmic dance moves which are arranged in a certain order to match with the beats of a song.

consumer (kuhn-SOO-mer)—A person who buys or uses a product or service.

gleefully (GLEE-fuhl-ee)—Happily; with great joy.

mainstream (MEYN-streem)—The widely accepted way of doing things; the trend.

poverty-striken (POV-er-tee-strik-uhn)—Having a significant population which is very poor.

Zumbathon (ZOOM-buh-thawn)—A Zumba exercise session (usually longer than the typical one-hour class) held for the purpose of raising money for charity.

All design elements from Thinkstock/Sharon Beck; Cover, p. 1—Photos.com/Thinkstock/Sharon Beck; p. 4—Monkey Business Images/Dreamstime; p. 6—Charles Trainor Jr/KRT/Newscom; pp. 8, 15, 20, 22, 26, 32-33—Dreamstime; p. 10—Walter Michot/MCT/Newscom; p. 11—Thinkstock; pp. 12, 41—Mikhail Grushin/Dreamstime; p. 16-17—The Washington Post/Getty Images; pp. 24-25—DDAA/ZOB WENN Photos/Newscom; p. 28— Clifford, Douglas R./ZUMApress/Newscom; p. 30—Angie Johnson Williams; p. 34—Susan Sokeland; p. 35—Lacey Johnson Wagner; p. 36—Angela Ostafichuk/Dreamstime; p. 38—SSE/ZDS WENN Photos/Newscom; p. 40—Alan Gignoux/Dreamstime

Index

About the Author

Michelle Medlock Adams is an award-winning author of sixty-four books including several titles for Mitchell Lane Publishers, and she is also a certified Zumba instructor. With an extensive dance and cheerleading background, Michelle found teaching fitness to be the perfect part-time job while she worked her way through journalism school at Indiana University. When Zumba came onto the fitness scene, Michelle jumped at the opportunity to get certified and lead classes at Priority Fitness in Bedford, Indiana. When she's not writing or leading fitness classes, Michelle enjoys cheering on the Indiana University Hoosiers, the Chicago Cubs, and the LA Kings. Find out more at her website: www.michellemedlockadams.com